To:

From:

Date:

199 Favorite Bible Verses for Women

© 2008 Christian Art Gifts Inc., IL, USA
Christian Art Publishers, RSA

First edition 2008
Second edition 2019

Designed by Christian Art Publishers

Images used under license from Shutterstock.com

Printed in China

ISBN 978-1-4321-3091-6

19 20 21 22 23 24 25 26 27 28 – 12 11 10 9 8 7 6 5 4 3

199
FAVORITE
BIBLE VERSES
for
Women

**CHRISTIAN ART
PUBLISHERS**

Contents

4. A Woman's Heart Reflects God's ...

5. Promises from God When I Experience ...

A Woman

Relies on God for His ...

*Put your hand into the
hand of God. He gives the
calmness and serenity
of heart and soul.*

~ Charles E. Cowman

A Woman Relies on God for His ...
Comfort

1

Blessed be the God and Father of
our Lord Jesus Christ, the Father of
mercies and God of all comfort, who
comforts us in all our tribulation.

2 Corinthians 1:3-4 NKJV

2

"I am leaving you with a gift – peace
of mind and heart. And the peace
I give is a gift the world cannot give.
So don't be troubled or afraid."

John 14:27 NLT

3

"As a mother comforts her child,
so will I comfort you."

Isaiah 66:13

Comfort

4

Cast your burden on the Lᴏʀᴅ, and
He shall sustain you; He shall never
permit the righteous to be moved.

Psalm 55:22 ɴᴋᴊᴠ

5

"Blessed are those who mourn, for
they shall be comforted."

Matthew 5:4 ᴇsᴠ

*It will greatly comfort you if you
can see God's hand in both
your losses and your crosses.*
~ Charles H. Spurgeon

A Woman Relies on God for His ...
Forgiveness

6

The Lord is faithful and just to
forgive us our sins and to cleanse us
from all unrighteousness.

1 John 1:9 NKJV

7

"Come now, let us reason together,
says the Lord: though your sins are like
scarlet, they shall be as white as snow;
though they are red like crimson,
they shall become like wool."

Isaiah 1:18 ESV

8

Oh, what joy for those whose
disobedience is forgiven,
whose sins are put out of sight.

Romans 4:7 NLT

9

"When you stand praying, if you hold anything against anyone, forgive him, so that your Father in heaven may forgive you your sins."

Mark 11:25

10

In Him we have redemption through His blood, the forgiveness of our trespasses, according to the riches of His grace.

Ephesians 1:7 ESV

To err is human, to forgive, divine.
~ Alexander Pope

A Woman Relies on God for His ...
Guidance

11

"I will instruct you and teach you in
the way you should go; I will guide
you with My eye."

Psalm 32:8 NKJV

12

God is our God for ever and ever;
He will be our guide even to the end.

Psalm 48:14

13

We can make our plans, but the LORD
determines our steps.

Proverbs 16:9 NLT

14

Trust in the L ORD with all your heart; do not depend on your own understanding. Seek His will in all you do, and He will show you which path to take.

Proverbs 3:5-6 NLT

15

Right behind you a voice will say, "This is the way you should go."

Isaiah 30:21 NLT

Hang this question up in your houses – "What would Jesus do?" and then think of another – "How would Jesus do it?" For what Jesus would do, and how He would do it, may always stand as the best guide to us.
~ Charles H. Spurgeon

A Woman Relies on God for His ...

Grace

16

"My grace is sufficient for you, for My power is made perfect in weakness."

2 Corinthians 12:9

17

The grace of the Lord Jesus Christ and the love of God and the fellowship of the Holy Spirit be with you all.

2 Corinthians 13:14 ESV

18

We believe that through the grace of the Lord Jesus Christ we shall be saved.

Acts 15:11 NKJV

19

God is able to make all grace abound
toward you, that you, always having all
sufficiency in all things, may have an
abundance for every good work.

2 Corinthians 9:8 NKJV

20

The grace of our Lord Jesus
be with you.

Romans 16:20

God doesn't just give us grace,
He gives us Jesus, the Lord of grace.
~ Joni Eareckson Tada

A Woman Relies on God for His ...
Provision

21

"Your Father knows the things you have
need of before you ask Him."

Matthew 6:8 NKJV

22

Take delight in the LORD, and He will
give you your heart's desires.

Psalm 37:4 NLT

23

God shall supply all your need
according to His riches in glory by
Christ Jesus. Now to our God and
Father be glory forever and ever. Amen.

Philippians 4:19-20 NKJV

Provision

24

Command those who are rich in
this present age not to be haughty,
nor to trust in uncertain riches
but in the living God, who gives
us richly all things to enjoy.

1 Timothy 6:17 NKJV

25

The Lord is my shepherd, I shall not
be in want. He makes me lie down in
green pastures, He leads me beside
quiet waters, He restores my soul.

Psalm 23:1-3

26

Let us not grow weary while doing
good, for in due season we shall
reap if we do not lose heart.

Galatians 6:9 NKJV

Abundance isn't God's provision for me to live in luxury, but His provision for me to help others live.

~ Randy Alcorn

Live today fully, expressing
gratitude for all you have been,
all you are right now,
and all you are becoming.

~ Melody Beattie

A Woman Relies on God for His ...
Redemptive Power

27

In Him we have redemption through
His blood, the forgiveness of sins,
in accordance with the riches of God's
grace that He lavished on us with
all wisdom and understanding.

Ephesians 1:7-8

28

The LORD will redeem those who
serve Him. No one who takes refuge
in Him will be condemned.

Psalm 34:22 NLT

29

Praise be to the Lord, the God
of Israel, because He has come
and has redeemed His people.

Luke 1:68

30

He has delivered us from the
domain of darkness and transferred
us to the kingdom of His beloved Son,
in whom we have redemption,
the forgiveness of sins.

Colossians 1:13-14 ESV

31

When the fullness of the time had
come, God sent forth His Son, born
of a woman, born under the law, to
redeem those who were under the law.

Galatians 4:4-5 NKJV

*One drop of Christ's blood is worth
more than heaven and earth.*

~ Martin Luther

God is my strong
salvation.
What foe have I
to fear?
In darkness and
temptation,
my light,
my help is near.

*A joyful heart is like the
sunshine of God's love,
the hope of eternal happiness,
a burning flame of God.
And if we pray, we will
become that sunshine of God's
love – in our own home,
the place where we live,
and in the world at large.*

~ Mother Teresa

A Woman Relies on God for His ...
Strength

32

"My grace is all you need.
My power works best in weakness."
So now I am glad to boast about my
weaknesses, so that the power of
Christ can work through me.

2 Corinthians 12:9 NLT

33

God is my strength and power,
and He makes my way perfect. He
makes my feet like the feet of deer,
and sets me on my high places.

2 Samuel 22:33-34 NKJV

34

God gives power to the faint,
and to him who has no might
He increases strength.

Isaiah 40:29 ESV

I pray also that the eyes of your heart may be enlightened in order that you may know the hope to which He has called you, and His incomparably great power for us who believe. That power is like the working of His mighty strength.

Ephesians 1:18-19

The way to grow strong in Christ is to become weak in yourself.
~ Charles H. Spurgeon

Wisdom

36

If you need wisdom, ask our generous
God, and He will give it to you.
He will not rebuke you for asking.

James 1:5 NLT

37

To the one who pleases Him God has
given wisdom and knowledge and joy.

Ecclesiastes 2:26 ESV

38

Joyful is the person who finds wisdom,
the one who gains understanding. For
wisdom is more profitable than silver,
and her wages are better than gold.

Proverbs 3:13-14 NLT

39

The fear of the LORD is the beginning
of wisdom; a good understanding have
all those who do His commandments.
His praise endures forever.

Psalm 111:10 NKJV

40

When she speaks, her words
are wise, and she gives
instructions with kindness.

Proverbs 31:26 NLT

41

Teach us to number our days aright,
that we may gain a heart of wisdom.

Psalm 90:12

The invariable mark
of wisdom is to
see the miraculous
in the common.

Once you loosen up,
let yourself be who you are:
the wonderful, witty woman whom
God will use to encourage
and uplift other people.

~ Barbara Johnson

What to Do
When I Need ...

God walks with us.
He scoops us up in His arms
or simply sits with us in silent strength
until we cannot avoid the awesome
recognition that yes,
even now, He is here.

~ Gloria Gaither

Assurance

42

"I am the LORD, your God, who takes
hold of your right hand and says to
you, 'Do not fear; I will help you.'"

Isaiah 41:13

43

Let us draw near with a true
heart in full assurance of faith.

Hebrews 10:22 NKJV

44

Give your burdens to the LORD,
and He will take care of you. He will
not permit the godly to slip and fall.

Psalm 55:22 NLT

Overwhelming victory is ours through Christ who loved us enough to die for us. For I am convinced that nothing can ever separate us from His love.

Romans 8:37-38 TLB

Blessed assurance, Jesus is mine!
Oh what a foretaste of Glory Divine!
Heir of salvation, purchase of God,
born of the Spirit, washed in His blood.
~ Fanny Crosby

What to Do When I Need ...
Courage

46

Be strong and courageous! Do not be
afraid or discouraged. For the LORD
your God is with you wherever you go.

Joshua 1:9 NLT

47

Be strong and do not give up,
for your work will be rewarded.

2 Chronicles 15:7

48

I can do everything through Christ,
who gives me strength.

Philippians 4:13 NLT

49

Be strong, and let your heart take
courage, all you who wait for the LORD!

Psalm 31:24 ESV

50

Be strong and of good courage,
do not fear nor be afraid of them;
for the LORD your God, He is the
One who goes with you. He will
not leave you nor forsake you.

Deuteronomy 31:6 NKJV

*Courage is an inner resolution to go
forward in spite of obstacles and
frightening situations.*
~ Martin Luther King, Jr

What to Do When I Need ...
Friendship

51

A friend loves at all times,
and a brother is born for adversity.

Proverbs 17:17 NKJV

52

"Greater love has no one
than this, that someone lay
down his life for his friends."

John 15:13 ESV

53

Perfume and incense bring joy to the
heart, and the pleasantness of one's
friend springs from his earnest counsel.

Proverbs 27:9

Friendship

54

Two are better than one, because
they have a good reward for their labor.
For if they fall, one will lift up
his companion. Though one may
be overpowered by another, two
can withstand him. And a threefold
cord is not quickly broken.

Ecclesiastes 4:9-10, 12 NKJV

55

Share each other's burdens, and in
this way obey the law of Christ.

Galatians 6:2 NLT

*A friend is able to see you as
the wonderful person God
created you to be.*

– Ann D. Parrish

What to Do When I Need ...
Hope

56

May the God of hope fill you with
all joy and peace in believing, so
that by the power of the Holy Spirit
you may abound in hope.

Romans 15:13 ESV

57

Let us hold fast the confession
of our hope without wavering,
for He who promised is faithful.

Hebrews 10:23 NKJV

58

Three things will last forever – faith,
hope, and love – and the greatest
of these is love.

1 Corinthians 13:13 NLT

59

Be of good courage, and He shall strengthen your heart, all you who hope in the LORD.

Psalm 31:24 NKJV

60

For You have been my hope, O Sovereign LORD, my confidence since my youth.

Psalm 71:5

Hope is the thing with feathers that perches in the soul, and sings the tunes without the words, and never stops at all.

~ Emily Dickinson

Peace

61

"I am leaving you with a gift – peace
of mind and heart. And the peace I
give is a gift the world cannot give.
So don't be troubled or afraid."

John 14:27 NLT

62

The peace of God, which surpasses all
understanding, will guard your hearts
and your minds in Christ Jesus.

Philippians 4:7 ESV

63

You will keep in perfect peace
all who trust in You, all whose
thoughts are fixed on You!

Isaiah 26:3 NLT

64

Let the peace of Christ rule in
your hearts, since as members of one
body you were called to peace.

Colossians 3:15

65

Therefore, having been justified
by faith, we have peace with God
through our Lord Jesus Christ.

Romans 5:1 NKJV

*We would have great peace
if we did not busy ourselves
with what others say and do.*
~ Thomas à Kempis

What to Do When I Need ...

Rest

66

Jesus said, "Come to Me, all of you who are weary and carry heavy burdens, and I will give you rest."

Matthew 11:28 NLT

67

"In returning and rest you shall be saved; in quietness and in trust shall be your strength."

Isaiah 30:15 ESV

68

Those who wait on the LORD shall renew their strength; they shall mount up with wings like eagles, they shall run and not be weary, they shall walk and not faint.

Isaiah 40:31 NKJV

69

"My Presence will go with you,
and I will give you rest."

Exodus 33:14 NKJV

70

My soul finds rest in God alone; my
salvation comes from Him. He alone
is my rock and my salvation; He is my
fortress, I will never be shaken.

Psalm 62:1-2

*Jesus knows that we must come
apart and rest a while, or else we
may just plain come apart.*

~ Vance Havner

Self-Control

71

Guard your heart above all else, for it
determines the course of your life.

Proverbs 4:23 NLT

72

Whoever guards his mouth and tongue
keeps his soul from troubles.

Proverbs 21:23 NKJV

73

Clothe yourselves with the Lord Jesus
Christ, and do not think about how to
gratify the desire of the sinful nature.

Romans 13:14

74

God gave us a spirit not of fear but of
power and love and self-control.

2 Timothy 1:7 ESV

75

Make every effort to add to your faith
goodness; and to goodness, knowledge; and to knowledge, self-control;
and to self-control, perseverance. For if
you possess these qualities in increasing
measure, they will keep you from being
ineffective and unproductive in your
knowledge of our Lord Jesus Christ.

2 Peter 1:5-6, 8

*Self-control is the mother
of spiritual wealth.*

~ John Climacus

If you are to be self-controlled in your speech, you must be self-controlled in your thinking.

~ François Fénelon

Trust the past to God's mercy, the present to God's love, and the future to God's providence.

~ Augustine of Hippo

Trust

76

"Do not let your hearts be troubled.
Trust in God; trust also in Me."

John 14:1

77

The LORD is good, a stronghold
in the day of trouble; and He
knows those who trust in Him.

Nahum 1:7 NKJV

78

Oh, the joys of those
who trust the LORD.

Psalm 40:4 NLT

79

Let the morning bring me
word of Your unfailing love,
for I have put my trust in You.

Psalm 143:8

80

Those who know Your name put their
trust in You, for You, O LORD, have not
forsaken those who seek You.

Psalm 9:10 ESV

*All God's giants have been
weak men who did great things
for God, because they believed
that God would be with them.*
~ Hudson Taylor

I love, my God, but with
no love of mine,
for I have none to give;
I love Thee, Lord,
but all the love is Thine,
for by Thy love I live.

~ Madame Jeanne Guyon

*All the blessings
we enjoy are divine
deposits, committed
to our trust on this
condition, that they
should be dispensed
for the benefits of
our neighbors.*

~ John Calvin

Popular Bible Verses
Concerning ...

I will not forget the benefits
of knowing God:
Unconditional love.
Forgiveness of sins.
Eternal salvation.
A second chance.
Peace beyond understanding.
Truth that sets me free.
Protection from the Evil One.
My daily bread.
The joy of the Lord.
And so much more.

~ Karla Dornacher

Blessings

81

The LORD bless you and keep you;
the LORD make His face to shine
upon you and be gracious to you;
the LORD lift up His countenance
upon you and give you peace.

Numbers 6:24-26 ESV

82

Open your mouth and taste, open
your eyes and see – how good GOD is.
Blessed are you who run to Him.

Psalm 34:8 THE MESSAGE

83

The LORD is my chosen portion and
my cup; You hold my lot. The lines
have fallen for me in pleasant places;
I have a beautiful inheritance.

Psalm 16:5-6 ESV

84

Bless the LORD, O my soul,
and forget not all His benefits,
who forgives all your iniquity,
who heals all your diseases,
who satisfies you with good
so that your youth is
renewed like the eagle's.

Psalm 103:2-3, 5 ESV

*God is more anxious to bestow
His blessings on us than we
are to receive them.*

~ Augustine of Hippo

85

"Have faith in God," Jesus answered. "I tell you the truth, if anyone says to this mountain, 'Go, throw yourself into the sea,' and does not doubt in his heart but believes that what he says will happen, it will be done for him."

Mark 11:22-23

86

It is impossible to please God without faith. Anyone who wants to come to Him must believe that God exists and that He rewards those who sincerely seek Him.

Hebrews 11:6 NLT

Faith is not believing that God can, but that God will.

87

Believe in the LORD your God, and you will be able to stand firm. Believe in His prophets and you will succeed.

2 Chronicles 20:20 NLT

88

Though you have not seen Him, you love Him. Though you do not now see Him, you believe in Him and rejoice with joy that is inexpressible and filled with glory, obtaining the outcome of your faith, the salvation of your souls.

1 Peter 1:8-9 ESV

Faith expects from God what is beyond all expectation.

~ Andrew Murray

89

How great is the love the Father
has lavished on us, that we should
be called children of God! And
that is what we are!

1 John 3:1

90

When I left the womb You
cradled me; since the moment
of birth You've been my God.

Psalm 22:10 THE MESSAGE

91

"I will be a Father to you, and you
will be My sons and daughters,
says the Lord Almighty."

2 Corinthians 6:18

92

As for me and my household,
we will serve the Lord.

Joshua 24:15

93

For this reason I bow my knees to
the Father of our Lord Jesus Christ,
from whom the whole family in
heaven and earth is named.

Ephesians 3:14-15 NKJV

*Children of the heavenly King,
as we journey let us sing;
sing our Savior's worthy praise,
glorious in His works and ways.*

~ John Cennick

Popular Bible Verses Concerning ...
God's Will

94

Give thanks in all circumstances;
for this is the will of God in
Christ Jesus for you.

1 Thessalonians 5:18 ESV

95

You need to persevere so that when
you have done the will of God, you
will receive what He has promised.

Hebrews 10:36

96

So if you are suffering according to
God's will, keep on doing what is right
and trust yourself to the God who
made you, for He will never fail you.

1 Peter 4:19 TLB

97

It is God who works in you, both to will
and to work for His good pleasure.

Philippians 2:13 ESV

98

Do not be conformed to this world,
but be transformed by the renewing
of your mind, that you may prove
what is that good and acceptable
and perfect will of God.

Romans 12:2 NKJV

*Inside the will of God
there is no failure.
Outside the will of God
there is no success.*

~ Bernard Edinger

Happiness

99

Happy are the people
whose God is the LORD.

Psalm 144:15 NKJV

100

A glad heart makes a happy face.

Proverbs 15:13 NLT

101

Joyful are those who have the God of
Israel as their helper, whose hope is in
the LORD their God. He made heaven
and earth, the sea and everything in
them. He keeps every promise forever.

Psalm 146:5-6 NLT

102

You have made known to me the
path of life; You will fill me with joy
in Your presence, with eternal
pleasures at Your right hand.

Psalm 16:11

*Laughter is the most beautiful
and beneficial therapy God
ever granted humanity.*
~ Charles Swindoll

Joy

103

You have put more joy in my
heart than they have when
their grain and wine abound.

Psalm 4:7 ESV

104

"If you keep My commandments, you
will abide in My love, just as I have kept
My Father's commandments and abide
in His love. These things I have spoken
to you, that My joy may remain in you,
and that your joy may be full."

John 15:10-11 NKJV

105

For our heart is glad in Him,
because we trust in His holy name.

Psalm 33:21 ESV

106

Those who sow in tears shall reap in joy.

Psalm 126:5 NKJV

107

Now may the God of hope fill you
with all joy and peace in believing,
that you may abound in hope by
the power of the Holy Spirit.

Romans 15:13 NKJV

108

The joy of the LORD is your strength.

Nehemiah 8:10

*Joy is the experience
of knowing
that you are
unconditionally loved.*

~ Henri Nouwen

The truths that I know best
I have learned on my knees.
I never know a thing well,
till it is burned into my
heart by prayer.

~ John Bunyan

109

The earnest prayer of a righteous
person has great power and
produces wonderful results.

James 5:16 NLT

110

The Lord is near to all who call on Him,
to all who call on Him in truth. He
fulfills the desires of those who fear
Him; He hears their cry and saves them.

Psalm 145:18-19

111

"Whatever you ask in prayer,
you will receive, if you have faith."

Matthew 21:22 ESV

112

"When you pray, go into your room, close the door and pray to your Father, who is unseen. Then your Father, who sees what is done in secret, will reward you."

Matthew 6:6

113

"I say to you, whatever things you ask when you pray, believe that you receive them, and you will have them."

Mark 11:24 NKJV

Only the prayer which comes from our hearts can get to God's heart.
~ Charles H. Spurgeon

114

"If two of you on earth agree about anything you ask for, it will be done for you by My Father in heaven. For where two or three come together in My name, there am I with them."

Matthew 18:19-20

115

Do not forsake your own friend or your father's friend, nor go to your brother's house in the day of your calamity; better is a neighbor nearby than a brother far away.

Proverbs 27:10 NKJV

116

Share each other's burdens, and in
this way obey the law of Christ.

Galatians 6:2 NLT

117

"Honor your father and mother" –
which is the first commandment with
a promise – "that it may go well
with you and that you may enjoy
long life on the earth."

Ephesians 6:2-3

*You can never establish a personal
relationship without opening
up your own heart.*

~ Paul Tournier

Success

118

"I know the plans I have for you,"
declares the LORD, "plans to prosper
you and not to harm you, plans to
give you hope and a future."

Jeremiah 29:11

119

Therefore be steadfast, immovable,
always abounding in the work of
the Lord, knowing that your labor
is not in vain in the Lord.

1 Corinthians 15:58 NKJV

120

Commit to the LORD whatever you do,
and your plans will succeed.

Proverbs 16:3

121

May the LORD give you the
desire of your heart and make
all your plans succeed.

Psalm 20:4

122

Our only power and success
comes from God.

2 Corinthians 3:5 TLB

*The only place where success
comes before work is in the dictionary.*
~ Vince Lombardi

I long to accomplish a great and noble task, but it is my chief duty to accomplish small tasks as if they were great and noble.

*For the heart
that finds joy
in small things,
in all things,
each day is a
wonderful gift.*

A Woman's Heart
Reflects God's ...

You may call God love,
you may call God goodness.
But the best name for God
is compassion.

~ Meister Eckhart

A Woman's Heart Reflects God's ...
Compassion

123

The LORD your God is gracious and compassionate. He will not turn His face from you if you return to Him.

2 Chronicles 30:9

124

Through the LORD's mercies we are not consumed, because His compassions fail not.

Lamentations 3:22 NKJV

125

The Lord is full of compassion and mercy.

James 5:11

126

The LORD is good to everyone. He
showers compassion on all His creation.

Psalm 145:9 NLT

127

Your compassion is great, O LORD;
preserve my life according to Your laws.

Psalm 119:156

*The best exercise for strengthening
the heart is reaching down and
lifting people up.*

— Ernest Blevins

128

Let your gentleness be known to all.
The Lord is at hand.

Philippians 4:5 NKJV

129

But the meek will inherit the
land and enjoy great peace.

Psalm 37:11

130

The fruit of the Spirit is love, joy, peace,
longsuffering, kindness, goodness,
faithfulness, gentleness, self-control.

Galatians 5:22-23 NKJV

131

Pursue righteousness and a godly life,
along with faith, love, perseverance,
and gentleness. Fight the good
fight for the true faith.

1 Timothy 6:11-12 NLT

132

You have given me the shield
of Your salvation, and Your
gentleness made me great.

2 Samuel 22:36 ESV

Nothing is so strong as gentleness,
nothing is so gentle as real strength.
~ Francis de Sales

A Woman's Heart Reflects God's ...

Honesty

133

If you weigh and measure things
honestly, the LORD your God will
let you enjoy a long life in the
land He is giving you.

Deuteronomy 25:15 CEV

134

Whatever is true, whatever is noble,
whatever is right, whatever is pure,
whatever is lovely, whatever is
admirable – if anything is excellent or
praiseworthy – think about such things.
And the God of peace will be with you.

Philippians 4:8-9

135

It is an honor to receive a frank reply.

Proverbs 24:26 TLB

136

Honesty lives confident and carefree,
but Shifty is sure to be exposed.

Proverbs 10:9 The Message

137

I know, my God, that You test the
heart and are pleased with integrity.
All these things have I given willingly
and with honest intent.

1 Chronicles 29:17

*Honesty is the first chapter
in the book of wisdom.*
~ Thomas Jefferson

Kindness

138

Since God chose you to be the holy
people He loves, you must clothe
yourselves with tenderhearted mercy,
kindness, humility, gentleness, and
patience. Remember, the Lord forgave
you, so you must forgive others.

Colossians 3:12-13 NLT

139

Who can find a virtuous wife?
For her worth is far above rubies.
She opens her mouth with wisdom,
and on her tongue is the law of
kindness. Charm is deceitful and
beauty is passing, but a woman who
fears the LORD, she shall be praised.

Proverbs 31:10, 26, 30 NKJV

140

Tell the LORD how thankful you are,
because He is kind and always merciful.

Psalm 118:1 CEV

141

His merciful kindness is great
toward us, and the truth of the
LORD endures forever.

Psalm 117:2 NKJV

*Kind words can be short
and easy to speak, but their
echoes are truly endless.*

~ Mother Teresa

Love

142

"For God so loved the world that
He gave His one and only Son,
that whoever believes in Him shall
not perish but have eternal life."

John 3:16

143

Eye has not seen, nor ear heard,
nor have entered into the heart of
man the things which God has
prepared for those who love Him.

1 Corinthians 2:9 NKJV

144

Love each other deeply, because
love covers over a multitude of sins.

1 Peter 4:8

145

I am persuaded that neither death nor life, nor angels nor principalities nor powers, nor things present nor things to come, nor height nor depth, nor any other created thing, shall be able to separate us from the love of God which is in Christ Jesus our Lord.

Romans 8:38-39 NKJV

146

Now these three remain: faith, hope and love. But the greatest of these is love.

1 Corinthians 13:13

The one who truly loves gives all and sacrifices nothing.
~ Rainer Maria Rilke

Patience

147

Wait for the LORD; be strong and
take heart and wait for the LORD.

Psalm 27:14

148

I waited patiently for the LORD;
He inclined to me and heard my cry.

Psalm 40:1 ESV

149

As God's chosen people, holy and
dearly loved, clothe yourselves
with compassion, kindness, humility,
gentleness and patience.

Colossians 3:12

150

The Lord is not slow in keeping His
promise, as some understand slowness.
He is patient with you, not wanting
anyone to perish, but everyone
to come to repentance.

2 Peter 3:9

151

Be patient and stand firm,
because the Lord's coming is near.

James 5:8

Patience with others is Love.
Patience with self is Hope.
Patience with God is Faith.

~ Adel Bestavros

A Woman's Heart Reflects God's ...
Perseverance

152

Consider it pure joy whenever you face
trials of many kinds, because you know
that the testing of your faith develops
perseverance. Perseverance must finish
its work so that you may be mature
and complete, not lacking anything.

James 1:2-4

153

Let us throw off everything that hinders
and the sin that so easily entangles,
and let us run with perseverance
the race marked out for us.

Hebrews 12:1

154

Be strong and do not let your hands be weak, for your work shall be rewarded!

2 Chronicles 15:7 NKJV

155

We rejoice in our sufferings, because we know that suffering produces perseverance; perseverance, character; and character, hope. And hope does not disappoint us, because God has poured out His love into our hearts by the Holy Spirit, whom He has given us.

Romans 5:3-5

156

You need to persevere so that when
you have done the will of God, you
will receive what He has promised.

Hebrews 10:36

157

"The one who endures
to the end will be saved."

Matthew 24:13 ESV

*Few things are impossible to diligence
and skill. Great works are performed,
not by strength, but by perseverance.*

~ Samuel Johnson

*God is a place
of safety you can run to,
but it helps if you are running
to Him on a daily basis so that
you are in familiar territory.*

~ Stormie Omartian

A Woman's Heart Reflects God's ...
Stability

158

Wisdom and knowledge will be
the stability of your times, and
the strength of salvation; the fear
of the LORD is His treasure.

Isaiah 33:6 NKJV

159

For if we are faithful to the end,
trusting God just as firmly as when
we first believed, we will share in
all that belongs to Christ.

Hebrews 3:14 NLT

160

Create in me a pure heart, O God,
and renew a steadfast spirit within me.

Psalm 51:10

161

Therefore, be steadfast, immovable,
always abounding in the work of
the Lord, knowing that in the
Lord your labor is not in vain.

1 Corinthians 15:58 ESV

162

The God of all grace, who called
you to His eternal glory in Christ,
will Himself restore you and make
you strong, firm and steadfast.

1 Peter 5:10

*Stability is found in
God's unfailing love.*

Truth

163

"When He, the Spirit of truth, comes,
He will guide you into all truth."

John 16:13

164

Jesus said to him, "I am the way, the
truth, and the life. No one comes to
the Father except through Me. If you
had known Me, you would have known
My Father also; and from now on you
know Him and have seen Him."

John 14:6-7 NKJV

165

Love does not delight in evil,
but rejoices with the truth.

1 Corinthians 13:6

166

Now that you have purified yourselves
by obeying the truth so that you
have sincere love for your brothers,
love one another deeply, from the heart.

1 Peter 1:22-23

167

Your justice is eternal, and Your
instructions are perfectly true.

Psalm 119:142 NLT

*Let us rejoice in the truth,
wherever we find its lamp burning.*
~ Albert Schweitzer

Where I found truth,
there I found my God,
who is the truth itself.
And thus since the time
I learned Thee, Thou abidest
in my memory; and there do
I find Thee whensoever I call
Thee to remembrance, and
delight in Thee.

~ Augustine of Hippo

To show great love for God
and our neighbor,
we need not do great things.
It is how much love we put
in the doing that makes
our offering something
beautiful for God.

~ Mother Teresa

Promises from God
When I Experience ...

When you accept rather than fight your circumstances, even though you don't understand them, you open your heart's gate to God's love, peace, joy, and contentment.

~ Amy Carmichael

Conflict

168

For our struggle is not against flesh and blood, but against the rulers, against the authorities, against the powers of this dark world and against the spiritual forces of evil in the heavenly realms. Therefore put on the full armor of God.

Ephesians 6:12-13

169

May the God who gives endurance and encouragement give you a spirit of unity among yourselves as you follow Christ Jesus, so that with one heart and mouth you may glorify the God and Father of our Lord Jesus Christ.

Romans 15:5-6

Conflict

170

You hide them in the shelter of Your presence, safe from those who conspire against them. You shelter them in Your presence, far from accusing tongues.

Psalm 31:20 NLT

171

When we were enemies we were reconciled to God through the death of His Son, much more, having been reconciled, we shall be saved by His life.

Romans 5:10 NKJV

172

When GOD approves of your life, even your enemies will end up shaking your hand.

Proverbs 16:7 THE MESSAGE

*The harder the conflict,
the more glorious
the triumph.*

*Be not angry that you
cannot make others as you
wish them to be,
since you cannot make
yourself as you wish to be.*

~ Thomas à Kempis

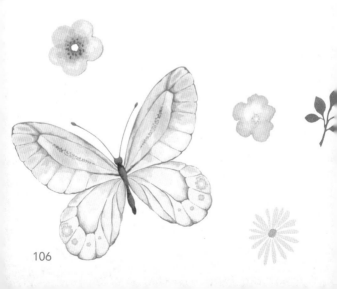

173

"Pray for the happiness of those
who curse you; implore God's
blessing on those who hurt you.
If someone slaps you on one cheek,
let him slap the other too!"

Luke 6:28-29 TLB

174

If you are insulted because of the name
of Christ, you are blessed, for the Spirit
of glory and of God rests on you.

1 Peter 4:14

175

Some people make cutting
remarks, but the words of
the wise bring healing.

Proverbs 12:18 NLT

176

"Blessed are you when others revile you and persecute you and utter all kinds of evil against you falsely on My account. Rejoice and be glad, for your reward is great in heaven."

Matthew 5:11-12 ESV

177

Rejoice that you participate in the sufferings of Christ, so that you may be overjoyed when His glory is revealed. If you are insulted because of the name of Christ, you are blessed.

1 Peter 4:13-14

Before you criticize someone, you should walk a mile in his shoes. That way, when you criticize him, you're a mile away and you have his shoes.

Disappointment

178

The LORD directs the steps of the godly. He delights in every detail of their lives. Though they stumble, they will never fall, for the LORD holds them by the hand.

Psalm 37:23-24 NLT

179

"When you pass through the waters, I will be with you; and when you pass through the rivers, they will not sweep over you. When you walk through the fire, you will not be burned; the flames will not set you ablaze. For I am the LORD, your God, the Holy One of Israel, your Savior."

Isaiah 43:2-3

180

Why are you cast down, O my soul?
And why are you disquieted within me?
Hope in God, for I shall yet praise Him
for the help of His countenance.

Psalm 42:5 NKJV

181

No matter how many times
you trip them up, God-loyal
people don't stay down long.

Proverbs 24:16 THE MESSAGE

182

Do not rejoice over me, my enemy;
when I fall, I will arise; when I sit in
darkness, the LORD will be a light to me.

Micah 7:8 NKJV

183

This hope will not lead to
disappointment. For we know
how dearly God loves us, because
He has given us the Holy Spirit
to fill our hearts with His love.

Romans 5:5 NLT

Expect people to be
better than they are;
it helps them to become better.
But don't be disappointed
when they are not;
it helps them to keep trying.
~ Mary Browne

No soul is desolate
as long as there is
a human being
for whom it
can feel trust
and reverence.

~ George Eliot

184

Even if my father and mother abandon me, the Lord will hold me close.

Psalm 27:10 NLT

185

"Behold, I am with you and will keep you wherever you go, and will bring you back to this land; for I will not leave you until I have done what I have spoken to you."

Genesis 28:15 NKJV

186

God sets the lonely in families.

Psalm 68:6

187

You are my hiding place;
You protect me from trouble. You
surround me with songs of victory.

Psalm 32:7 NLT

188

For I am persuaded that neither death
nor life, nor angels nor principalities nor
powers, nor things present nor things
to come, nor height nor depth, nor any
other created thing, shall be able to
separate us from the love of God
which is in Christ Jesus our Lord.

Romans 8:38-39 NKJV

*Loneliness is the first thing which
God's eye named not good.*

~ John Milton

Promises from God When I Experience ...

Stress

189

"Come to Me, all you who
labor and are heavy laden,
and I will give you rest."

Matthew 11:28 NKJV

190

Give your burdens to the L<small>ORD</small>,
and He will take care of you. He will
not permit the godly to slip and fall.

Psalm 55:22 NLT

191

Those who trust in the L<small>ORD</small> are
like Mount Zion, which cannot
be shaken but endures forever.

Psalm 125:1

192

You keep him in perfect peace
whose mind is stayed on You,
because he trusts in You.

Isaiah 26:3 ESV

193

"Do not worry, saying, 'What shall
we eat?' or 'What shall we drink?'
or 'What shall we wear?' For the
pagans run after all these things,
and your heavenly Father knows
that you need them."

Matthew 6:31-32

*One of the best ways to counteract
stress is to pray for others.*

194

"Seek first the kingdom of God and
His righteousness, and all these things
shall be added to you. Therefore
do not worry about tomorrow,
for tomorrow will worry about its
own things. Sufficient for the
day is its own trouble."

Matthew 6:33-34 NKJV

195

Do not be anxious about anything,
but in everything, by prayer and
petition, with thanksgiving, present
your requests to God. And the
peace of God, which transcends all
understanding, will guard your hearts
and your minds in Christ Jesus.

Philippians 4:6-7

196

For God did not give us a spirit of
timidity, but a spirit of power,
of love and of self-discipline.

2 Timothy 1:7

197

Give all your worries and cares
to God, for He cares about you.

1 Peter 5:7 NLT

198

Cast your burden on the LORD,
and He shall sustain you;
He shall never permit the
righteous to be moved.

Psalm 55:22 NKJV

199

My friends, you must do all you can to show that God has really chosen and selected you. If you keep on doing this, you won't stumble and fall.

2 Peter 1:10 CEV

Never try to carry tomorrow's burdens with today's grace.

My own favorite Bible verses ...

My own favorite Bible verses ...

Notes

These extra pages have been provided for your personal reflections and notes ...

_____

_____

_____

_____

_____

_____

_____

_____

_____

_____

_____

_____

_____

_____

_____

_____

_____

_____

_____

_____

_____

_____

Notes

Notes

Notes